EMAIL MARKETING PRO

A Beginner's Guide To Writing Emails That Sell

Paraic Bergin
Foreword by Matt Bacak

Lodestone Publishing

CONTENTS

Title Page

Copyright

Foreword by Matt Bacak

Introduction

Who Are You Anyway? — 1

What Is Your Goal? — 4

Your Ideal Customer Profile — 7

Write To Your Ideal Customer — 12

Use Your Authentic Voice — 14

Write Good Subject Lines — 19

Write Emails People Want To Read — 21

Consistent Messaging — 36

Bonus: Nine ways to write Winning Subject Lines — 42

Bonus: Tracking & Testing — 48

About The Author — 57

FOREWORD BY MATT BACAK

When Paraic Bergin asked me to write the Foreword to his latest book, I nearly said no.

I mean, I get a lot of requests. I can't say yes to them all. Even if I wanted to. Even if the books were good enough.

Then I read it, and changed my mind.

I've known Paraic for a few years. He was a student on my three day 'Email Millionaire Intensive'. He came with a small list of Zombie subscribers - no engagement, no sales. He wanted to start at the beginning and learn how to do it right.

So, written by a guy who's not afraid to admit his mistakes - by a guy who learns from them - this is the absolute perfect book to read if you are dreaming of making real money online.

Because the best way to make real money online is email marketing. And that means sending emails that get opened, that get engagement, that get clicks.

This short book is one of the best 'beginners' guides I've seen.

Read it. Enjoy it. Apply it. Profit from it.

Matt Bacak

Digital Marketing Legend

http://aboutmattbacak.com/

INTRODUCTION

Consider the following for a moment...

You've done a wonderful job of building your list and now have a focused list of subscribers who are impatiently expecting your next email.

You want to convert new subscribers into committed readers who will open each and every email you send them in the future.

But...guess what? It doesn't turns out like that.

This is where a lot of email marketers fall down.

They build the list, but don't keep readers engaged. Subscribers read the first few messages, but then fade away.

Without re-engagement or some kind of reward, they'll ultimately quit and unsubscribe.

Worse, they'll stay on your list depressing your open and click-thru rates and costing you money.

Why?

Simple. You're not giving them what they want.

Although writing seems to be straightforward, there are several elements that must be combined to create a good email that can grab and hold your readers attention, and keep them coming back for more.

And that is exactly what this little book is about.

We're going to look at the critical components of an effective email, from appealing subject lines to engaging content to the technological variables that make a difference.

By the time we're finished, you'll know exactly what you need to do (and how to do it) so your subscribers will open and read your email, and look forward to your next one.

Chapters 1 – 3 are all about you – who you are, your goals and your ideal subscriber.

Chapters 4 – 5 are about your audience – writing to and for one person, developing and using your authentic voice

Chapters 6 – 8 are about your message – from subject lines to writing emails people want to read and consistent messaging.

Let's get started.

WHO ARE YOU ANYWAY?

Imagine a group of prospects who are all keen on investments.

Paraic Bergin emails half of these prospects. The other half get a Warren Buffett email.

Which email do you think these prospects will open first?

That's correct, they'll read Warren Buffett's investing advice.

They might not even open Paraic Bergin's email if they don't recognize my name as a finance-pro.

People want to follow experts. They deliberately seek out niche experts to follow.

That's why you'll need to develop your own skills.

Essentially, you need to become the "Go-To-Expert" in your niche, which will automatically increase your followers.

How To Be Recognized As An Expert

- <u>Demonstrate your expertise.</u>
  The best way to prove your expertise is to simply show your audience that you know your stuff. To put it another way, if you provide unique material, people will naturally see you as an authority in your field.

- <u>Emphasize your skills.</u>
Show off your qualifications if you have them to prove you're an expert. That doesn't imply you talk about yourself (as you need to create content centered around your readers, not you). But you should occasionally remind them why they should listen to you.

What Kind Of Credentials? Among Them:

- <u>A relevant degree.</u>
If you're writing about relieving back pain, mention if you have a related degree like nursing.

- <u>Work experience in a relevant field.</u>
If you teach people how to sell their homes for more money, you might mention your 25 years as a real estate agent.

- <u>Results proof (for yourself and others).</u>
If you work with folks who want to lose weight, exhibit "before" and "after" photos of clients who have lost weight under your guidance.

- <u>Field accolades and awards.</u>
If you teach people how to write bestselling novels, show them your writing awards.

Other Ways To Gain Recognition:

- <u>Make yourself available for interviews.</u>
Marketers sometimes try to get experts to speak on their

webinars. That helps in various ways. But if you want to be viewed as an authority in your field, you should conduct interviews on webinars, podcasts, and talk radio.

- <u>Host your own podcast and interview others.</u>
You could do this every month. Others in your niche will seek you to be their guest once they hear your interviews.

- <u>Write a book.</u>
You can publish it on Amazon. It doesn't have to be a big book, or sell lots of copies (although that's great too!). But the point is, people think only experts write books and if you're an author, they'll regard you as an expert.

- <u>Guest blogging.</u>
People will naturally see you as an authority if your content appears on many (popular) blogs in your industry.

What it comes down to is consumers want to read emails from experts. So building your reputation and raising your profile will increase your open and response rates.

WHAT IS YOUR GOAL?

<u>Start with the end in mind - Steven Covey</u>

Before you even begin to consider drafting a single word of your email, you should first identify the specific reason for sending it.

And there should only be ONE reason.

If you're trying to accomplish several objectives in one email, all you end up with is a weak message and a confused reader.

Russel Brunson, CEO of ClickFunnels, will tell you a confused customer buys nothing.

Confronted with too many things to think about, your readers may decide to take no action at all.

Of course there are occasions when a message may accomplish more than one objective.

A good sales letter for example will answer objections and build familiarity or trust.

And your email may help you establish a stronger connection with your readers.

However, it's best to narrow your focus. Have one aim, and then write your email to lead to that goal.

So, what kind of goals should we have?

Here Are A Few Suggestions:

1. <u>Selling your own product or service</u>
Your message could include information, case studies, promo material, etc.

2. <u>Selling someone else's product or service</u>
The vast majority of online sales are through affiliates. You need to be able to compete with other affiliates and your emails will include not only vendor sales and marketing materials but also your own created content. This may be a review of the product, bonuses you are offering, etc.

3. <u>Pre-selling - overt</u>
In pre-launch marketing, you want to create a sense of excitement and expectation.

4. <u>Pre-selling – covert</u>
You may want your reader to subscribe to a someone else's list or for a subscription where you will earn or gain a benefit or reward.

5. <u>Drive traffic to your website</u>
Send your readers to a blog post, video or other promo.

6. <u>Drive traffic to another site</u>
E.g. to social media for likes and/or follows.

7. <u>Gather feedback and/or identify niche interests</u>

This is free market research, made more powerful by the fact you already have a relationship with them. Ask your readers to 'put their hand up' so you can gauge the potential in sub-niches.

8. Build reputation

Use your emails to establish and reinforce your position in the market.

9. Updates and news

Important news and events that may affect your subscribers.

While these are some of the most common objectives this is by no means an exhaustive list.

The key thing is to decide what you want to accomplish <u>before</u> you start writing.

YOUR IDEAL CUSTOMER PROFILE

This isn't a game of chance. You don't make this decision based on your fantasies about the type of consumer you want to serve.

Instead, you create a customer avatar that is based on the actual person who is your customer.

This demands a little research and some thought:

- Pay attention to your prospects and customers in order to gain a deeper understanding of who they are.

- Take note of what they're saying on your blog (or similar blogs), in social media, and in discussion groups or forums, and act on it.

- Communicate with them directly in order to have a better understanding of their problems, desires, and motivations.

- Engage in their activities for a short while. This will help you gain a deeper understanding, e.g. for get-fit enthusiasts, adopt a get-fit lifestyle yourself, including going to your local gym/fitness center/walking/running track and mingling with the others there.

- Conduct surveys of your target audience. Begin with a survey of your current list to learn more about who they are in terms of demographics, as well as what they want, what they've tried, where their "pain points" are, and so on. After that, you can branch out and survey your market segments in other locations, such as social media and other online forums, if necessary.

- Research your target audience. Other institutions (such as the government, research groups, and universities) may choose to make their research available to the general public in specific instances. This is one method of obtaining demographic information as well as views and viewpoints from respondents.

The more you understand your target audience, the more effectively you will be able to communicate with them.

Answer These Questions:

- Gender?

- Age?

- Income?

- Where does s/he live?

- Owner or tenant?

- Has spouse/partner?

- Children?

- Educational background?

- Income range?

- Career?

- Hobbies?

- Problems?

Consider specific pain points or challenges you can help with

Solutions s/he has tried in the past?

Why those solutions haven't been successful?

Also:

Blogs, specialized magazines, and other resources s/he reads/follows?

His/her level of expertise in the niche - novice, intermediate or expert?

What is it that the prospect is looking for?

What drives them to do what they do?

What is it that they are afraid of?

And everything else you can uncover about your prospects that will assist you in building a relationship with them.

<u>Take the case of young moms with toddlers:</u>

Say you conduct some preliminary investigation and discover that the majority of these mothers are really busy.

Employed full-time. Raising two children, both of whom are now enrolled in pre-school.

Also devotes a significant amount of time to transporting these children to and from play-dates, social activities, appointments, events, and so on.

This mom want to get fit again and recover the figure she had before the kids were born.

But she doesn't have a lot of free time on her hands.

Certainly doesn't have time to prepare separate dinners — one for herself and another that is "tastier" and that her family will genuinely like eating.

Her schedule also doesn't allow her to dedicate a great deal of time and energy to working out.

You may establish a connection with this potential prospect by empathizing with their hectic schedule.

E.g. "I understand what it's like to be a busy parent — it feels like all you do is taxi your children to events, clean up after them, and assist them with their homework.

Although you are keen to slim down and get fit again, there are occasions when it appears that you simply don't have the necessary time or enthusiasm."

You can also provide solutions that are tailored to their hectic schedule.

For example, "These low-calorie recipes are so tasty that the whole family will enjoy them, so you won't have to cook two meals any longer. In addition, they're quick to prepare, with each one requiring an average of 15 minutes of preparation time."

It is only after you have a clear understanding of your target customer that you will be able to design content that will truly resonate with them.

However, you'll also need to understand how to generate material that captivates your readers and keeps them engaged throughout the reading process.

And that brings us to…

WRITE TO YOUR IDEAL CUSTOMER

If you try to write for everyone, you'll wind up writing to no one.

That's the bottom line. That is why you must write your emails in the first person for your target consumer.

Imagine for a minute that you have subscribers who are all trying to get fit.

And for arguments sake, let's say you already have a few different audience segments in your mind.

Perhaps you have "moms with toddlers" as well as early 20's males, and even some middle aged men and women.

They're all looking for exercise and fitness suggestions, and answers to their problems.

Now, if you try to write to these different groups at the same time, you will find that you won't resonate with any of them.

You'll probably find they won't even respond to you because you don't seem to understand them, their needs and desires .

Because, let's face it, their motives and reasons are quite different. Furthermore, their lives differ markedly.

Therefore your recommendations have to take this into consideration.

So figure out who your IDEAL client or customer is. Then write for and to that person, and that person only.

Now, I get the fear: if you write for a certain audience, you run the risk of alienating anyone who doesn't fit the profile.

For example:

Young men in their 20's will generally have very different fitness goals than young mothers with small kids. You can't give each of them the same message – you have to create unique messages for these groups.

So, what exactly happens?

When you write to a certain segment of your audience, you wind up reducing the size of your group.

That's actually the point – that's what you're aiming for.

Because when you narrow your focus, you attract the attention of your ideal customers while simultaneously repelling the attention of everyone else.

The end result is that you have a list that is highly targeted and highly responsive!

With that in mind, here's what you should do next...

USE YOUR AUTHENTIC VOICE

Email marketers have a tendency to send inconsistent emails. The "voice" may be erratic.

In certain circumstances, the messaging is disjointed.

Readers are turned off in either case... they quit opening your emails... They may also unsubscribe in some situations.

So, let's talk about your authentic voice and how to maintain consistency...

Consistent Voice

The general "flavor" of your message is determined by your voice. This is how you communicate your message.

Consider other marketing messages you've seen, or simply go through your email inbox.

You'll notice that different marketers have different "voices."

Part of this is due to the marketer's unique writing style.

However, the second component that contributes to the voice is a deliberate attempt to give your brand a voice.

As a result, you must ask yourself, "What type of voice best complements your brand?"

For example, if you have a fun and light brand, your message voice should be fun and light as well.

Be conversational, use humor, and have some fun with your readers.

Consider whether your brand is serious.

In such instance, your messaging will ideally be professional, instructive, and confident.

What if your brand is about helping busy folks succeed?

Then make sure your messaging is tight and succinct.

There is no fluff or filler here, simply a solid message that busy individuals can read, digest, and apply quickly.

The point is, stop for a moment and consider your brand.

What are one or two adjectives that best characterize your brand?

And how will you convey your brand's message through your messaging?

What you'll want to do is list the adjectives that best reflect the tone of voice you'll employ for your messaging.

For example: confident... sarcastic... serious... witty... professional... helpful... educational... and so on.

Then, whenever you sit down to write an email, double-check that your wording meets those adjectives.

It's also a good idea to produce an email style guide (and for all your messaging across platforms).

This is especially true if you are not the sole creator of the content.

If you're working with business partners, workers, or independent contractors to create content, make sure you're all writing in the same tone.

When it comes to writing, you'll need to think about a lot of the finer things, as all of these small details contribute to your messaging voice.

You'll need to establish your voice in terms of these specifics, which you should then document in a style guide.

Consider The Following:

• Do you use a lot of exclamation points, or none at all? When do you utilize them if you do? (Give examples of when you'll most likely use them.)

• Do you employ industry jargon or acronyms? If so, when do you put them to use? When you use them, do you explain what they mean and why you're using them?

• Do you use profanity in your emails? If so, which ones are permissible? In what context do you employ them? How frequently do you employ them? (For example, sparingly or generously?)

• What is your content's overall format? What about long form? Short hints? How about step-by-step instructions with links to more resources? Images or graphics? (And what kind of visuals do you use?)

• What kind of writing style will work best for your audience? Should your content, for example, always be grammatically correct? Or do you like to breach the rules on purpose, such as by using a sentence fragment for emphasis? When is it OK to break the rules?

• What is your audience's level of expertise in the niche? For example, beginning, intermediate, or advanced?

• What else do you know about the reader that will help you develop material that will resonate with them? (Think about the research you did for developing your ideal customer avatar.)

As you can see, there are many aspects to think about while creating a style guide.

Go over your existing (effective) material to see what styles you've been employing that have worked for you so far.

If you're creating this guide for others, make sure to include links to your existing material that demonstrate all of the above ideas.

Let's assume you're defining when it's okay to use swear words in your material:

- First, expressly define and explain when this terminology is permissible to use.

-   Then, to demonstrate your case, show your partners and freelancers instances of your content where you

thought these terms were appropriate and even impactful (as well as content where you concluded there would be no value in using such words).

Don't leave people guessing what you mean.

Instead, provide examples so they understand exactly what you're looking for in terms of voice and style.

Now that you've defined your audience and your voice, it's time to look at the message itself...

WRITE GOOD SUBJECT LINES

We won't try to whitewash it: bad email subject lines equal bad open rates.

Sure, you can compensate for a bad subject line by building strong relationships with your subscribers.

But even if you have that, you still want intriguing subject lines to increase your open rates.

So, what constitutes a decent subject line?

Several Things Make Readers Click, Including...

- Curiosity.
  It's like giving your readers an itch that they can only scratch by opening your email. "No one tells you the #1 fat-loss secret..."

- Urgency.
  Basically, it's a fear of missing out (FOMO). "Last chance to join the webinar..."

- Freebies.
  Free is a potent trigger word. "FREE nutrition consultation if

you act now..."

- Solutions.
  This subject line provides a simple solution to a prospect's pressing issue. "Do the Shake and Vac to get the freshness back..."

- Personalization.
  Including your reader's name in the email might be very effective. "Jim, here's your coupon..."

- Name calling.
  To draw attention, name a renowned person (dead or alive). For example, "Not even the Queen of England knows this..."

Once you have a subject line that brings your reader in, the next thing is to look at the email itself...

WRITE EMAILS PEOPLE WANT TO READ

This is a multi-faceted problem that's made up of a number of smaller issues.

Let's look at what goes into crafting emails that people want to open and read:

Keeping In Touch

Your relationship with your subscribers is a major factor in whether or not they open, read, and respond to your emails.

Do they recognize you? Like and respect? Trust and believe in you?

Take a look at the people you know in person. To build a strong relationship with someone, you must talk to them on a regular basis.

The same holds true for your subscribers.

Sending emails on a regular basis is essential if you want to cultivate meaningful connections with other people (at least weekly if not more).

This not only aids in relationship building, but it also raises your visibility in people's minds.

If you rely on your autoresponder to nurture your relationship with your customers, use evergreen content.

Avoid references that age, go stale or quickly become irrelevant.

Every problem or issue has core, persistent factors as well as durable and lasting solutions.

Make sure there is an evergreen nature to the solutions and items you recommend.

Give Them What They Desire

Providing your readers with what they want is another approach to establish strong bonds with them (and boost open rates).

There are three approaches to discover what they desire.

Rather than relying solely on one of these strategies, consider combining all three:

1. <u>The first step is to do some research on your market:</u> Find out what your competitors are doing in terms of both free and paid content. Then, describe a similar (yet better) solution.

2. <u>Ask your readers themselves:</u>

You may learn more about their pain points and issues by conducting a survey and incorporating their feedback into your mailings. Also ask them directly about the content and solutions they'd like to see from you.

3. <u>Analyze your results:</u>
Keep track of the kind of material that is most popular with your subscribers so that you can continue to provide them with more.

This isn't only about the subject matter, but includes the general presentation as well.

Do they prefer long-form articles or shorter tips, for example?

A product review vs. an ad targeting them directly?

Tracking their responses over time will help you discover trends that reveal what they want.

Give Them Great Content, And Lots Of It

If you want your readers to stick around, you should present a wide range of content, including long-term solutions.

In addition to this, you'll want to make sure you're providing actionable information.

Your readers should be able to put this information to good use right away and see results in a short period of time.

Here's an illustration...

Most people's journey to a healthier weight involves numerous setbacks, fall-backs and relapses.

At one pound a week, it will take six months to lose 26 pounds, assuming no slip-ups.

To help people achieve this final aim, your information and solutions should keep the long term goal in sight.

And it's also a good idea to include quick fixes and pointers that can be implemented right away.

Simple processes that can be completed in under ten minutes are ideal so long as they also help them achieve their long-term objectives.

People who see results quickly tend to feel more energized and happier. They'll feel accomplished and proud of their progress as a result.

This means that as soon as they finish the task, they can start enjoying the rewards.

The point is that individuals will feel great when they take action and obtain fantastic outcomes.

So, be sure to include stuff that your readers can act on.

The Abc Method (Always Be Closing)

Some email marketers believe that they must first "nurture" their subscribers before they can begin promoting their products and services.

"Giving" before "getting" is a common sentiment.

That's admirable, to be sure.

Unfortunately, if you don't promote something as soon as your subscribers sign up, you're merely educating them to expect free material and solutions.

People will not be offended if you propose things when they know that you will offer both free and paid solutions.

There are a few additional things to keep in mind...

Your subscribers are interested in what you have to say and how you might help them.

They'll naturally expect that you'll only recommend the BEST options.

Make sure to meet these expectations.

There is no reason to delay a solution because it costs money.

Imagine a person with a painful condition, e.g. chronic back pain. Let's say the best option you've found isn't free.

Are you going to make your readers suffer by keeping them in the dark about this option because you believe you should "nurture your list" first?

Your reader would continue to suffer as a result.

You should be marketing from the beginning, since failing to do so will almost certainly result in you withholding your greatest value.

Build A Reputation For Honesty & Integrity

Even though it should be obvious, many marketers fail to remember that they must always be honest and professional with their audience.

People will lose faith in you if they discover that you are not being truthful.

After that, you'll have a hard time getting them to open your emails (much less respond to them).

We are conditioned to expect, and to a degree to accept, dishonesty.

<u>Salespeople and politicians hold the top 5 places in the Gallup poll of dishonest professions.</u>

Some people now regards telling 'white lies' as OK, in much the same way as most employees feel it is fine to take office supplies home from work.

But making claims that aren't true erodes trust in the whole marketing process.

False scarcity methods are frequently employed by marketers.

The special offer that must end at midnight for example.

But then it doesn't end.

You return the next day and see the offer hasn't changed, it's still at the same price.

I'm sure we've all seen something like that.

The bottom line is this:

You lose credibility, trust, and future sales if you engage in this type of behavior.

If you promote poor products, you're doing yourself and your customers more harm than good.

If a product you're reviewing is truly unsatisfactory, explain why you believe there are better options available.

If you exaggerate the benefits, or ignore the problems you'll pay for it afterwards.

Make sure you're being honest with your readers.

All of these little things add up when you're trying to establish trust with your customers.

Create Excitement

Every email you send should aim to arouse curiosity, ideally in both of the following ways:

1. The email should capture the reader's attention and make them interested in what's to come.

2. The reader should be eagerly anticipating what's to come in the next message.

So a key element to consider when writing emails that people want to read is producing interesting and engaging content.

New and useful information on its own isn't enough. Because here's the deal...

People don't generally read. And when they do, they don't want to be bored to death.

The average American reads at a Grade 8 level.

Even the World Health Organization and the US Center for Disease Control publish their information at this reading level to make sure it can be understood.

On top of that, people's ability to focus and concentrate is falling.

A 2015 Microsoft study found the average attention span <u>reduced from 12 to 8 seconds</u> since the start of the new millennium.

Whether there is any causal relationship between the decline in our attention span and the rise in the use of digital technology, and smartphones in particular, the fact remains that you have literally seconds to hook your reader.

It makes no difference if you're presenting your niche's holy grail.

It makes no difference if you've done an excellent job of establishing yourself as an expert.

If your content is dry and your subscribers see you as boring, your open and response rates will suffer.

So you have to deliver good quality content that engages the reader right from the start.

Pointers For More Engaging Emails:

- <u>Storytelling</u>
People love stories. Make them interesting. Get your reader emotionally invested.

- <u>Use humor</u>
However, comedy is subjective and tastes vary widely across cultures. Make sure you understand your audience.

- <u>Use shock</u>
Controversy is a great way to engage your readers. But as with humor, you need to know your audience.

- <u>Write in the first person</u>
As if you were speaking to a friend. Avoid using big words, keep to a casual style of writing.

- <u>Use suspense</u>
Make your reader curious, e.g. "In a moment, I'll reveal a little-known technique that can double your conversion rates. But first..."

- <u>Use analogies, metaphors, and similes</u>
Don't simply state the bald facts. Describe things in ways that create pictures in your reader's mind's eye.

- <u>Use different writing styles</u>
Vary your writing between long and short sentences. Match the writing to the theme e.g. long and lazy vs short, sharp shock. Short three-word sentences create tension. Look at how fiction writers employ these devices to create and sustain atmosphere.

Be Memorable

If you want your subscribers to open and read your emails on a regular basis, you not only must make them worth the effort, you must make yourself memorable.

To stand out from the crowd, you need to be seen as unique. This positioning sets you apart from your competitors.

The uniqueness extends to your content as well.

Consider this...

How long do you think a new subscriber will remain around if she opens your first few emails and reads content that she can get elsewhere?

The core content itself doesn't have to be unique to you.

But your content must contain something worthwhile that is unique, whether that's your opinion, or an insider view, or an expert analysis, or a ho-holds-barred review, etc.

Think about your favourite news or YouTube channel, social media influencer, coffee shop even.

Think about why you prefer that particular one.

Much the same rules apply to your own content and positioning.

Now, just because you're giving something fresh doesn't mean every email has to be packed with ground-breaking strategies that no one in your niche has ever heard of.

It's great to be able to pioneer tactics in your area, and you should aspire to do so, but it's not a must for getting

people to access, read, and respond to your content on a constant basis.

To succeed at that, you need to understand your environment, the content ecosystem and your place in it.

To begin, subscribe to and read your competitors' emails on a regular basis.

Look at their content on other platforms, such as their blogs and social media pages, while you're at it.

Examine their social media 'likes,' 'comments' and 'shares' to get a sense of how popular a topic is.

Buy and test their products.

The benefits of this are twofold:

1. <u>You get to see what's hot in your field</u>
If numerous competitors in your niche are sending out information on the same issue, it's a sign that the topic is popular. These are the kinds of issues you'll want to discuss.

2. <u>You get to see how your competitors approach it.</u>
How are they discussing it, teaching it?

This is where the uniqueness and difference come into play...

Your aim is to express it differently than your competitors now that you know what they're saying.

Teach Things In A New Way

Bear in mind that you're not sending every email to compete with everyone else in your market.

Instead, concentrate on being unique and continually seeking to improve.

Compete against yourself, and just look at your own numbers to see how well you're doing.

You might be asking how exactly you teach material in a fresh method at this stage.

You'll notice a lot of easy "step-by-step" articles if you look at what others in your industry are doing.

Here are some ideas for making your material more distinctive (without needing to try completely new approaches):

Make Up New Phrases

Inventing new words or phrases for things is one method to make your material stand out.

Take, for example, a standard opt-in (lead) page. Because no one had a decent name for it, it was commonly referred to as an opt-in page. That was both descriptive and effective.

Then one marketer coined the term "squeeze page," and the term caught on.

And you can bet that the marketer's reputation in the sector was enhanced, and a large number of subscribers became devoted fans.

Acronyms/Formulas

If everyone in your area is offering step-by-step instructions, see if you can put this "how to" material into a formula.

Let me give you an illustration:

Attention, Interest, Desire, and Action (AIDA)

AIDA is an acronym that properly captures the essential framework of a sales letter and is far easier to use than

Step 1: Attract Attention.
Step 2:...

Now consider your own teaching niche and topics. What formulas or acronyms can you use to distinguish yourself from the competition?

Use Ideas From Other Niches

It's fantastic if you can be the first to implement new tactics and share them with your subscribers. If not, have a look at what other niches are doing and see if you can apply any of their techniques to your own.

E.g: Did you know that the standard operating procedures for fast food service and kitchen cleanliness were devised from airline pilots' pre-flight safety checklists?

Alternatively, you might just put a new spin on an old technique. E.g. variations of low-carb diets.

Case Studies And Test Results

If you check around your niche, you'll probably find that a lot of email publishers focus on how to write content. If that's the case, here's another opportunity to set yourself apart.

You'll build a strong following by going the extra mile. Try tactics in your niche and report back on the results (whether expected or unexpected).

If you're catering to a weight-loss audience, for example, put eating techniques, exercises, and supplements to the test.

Don't just state, "This diet's cuisine is tasty and will help you lose weight."

Rather, find volunteers to follow the diet and keep meticulous records of their weight, measurements, emotions, hunger levels, and other factors.

You'll be able to share information that only a few others in your field can, and you can guarantee that will set you apart.

Provide Resources

Many email publishers focus on providing directions for completing a process, but they don't provide tools (apart from purchased items) to make the process easier. You may differentiate yourself from your competition by providing tools that encourage individuals to act and achieve better results.

These are some of the tools:

• Checklists • Worksheets • Mind maps

• Cheat sheets • Templates • Swipes

• Lists (such as gear lists) • Planners

• Calculators • Apps

If you teach copywriting, for example, you might include resources like:

- An audience profiling worksheet in your newsletters.
- A check-list for sales letters.
- A template for a sales letter.
- Email swipe files
- and so on.

If you're helping someone who wants to lose weight, you could add resources like:

- A calculator for calculating how many calories to consume.
- A workout scheduler.
- A series of food suggestions.
- Grocery lists.
- A journal template

... as well as similar goods.

So, you get the idea—if you can get your email subscribers to act, they'll receive terrific results. And when they get good results, they become devoted subscribers.

CONSISTENT MESSAGING

You And Your Reader

Your reader may recognize your name in the "from" field, but may not feel they know you well enough to open your emails.

Not everything in an email is going to be what the reader wants.

Some things that can go into having a good relationship with your subscribers include giving them content they can't get anywhere else, being honest with them, and trying to help them.

Another thing to think about is what kind of expectations you've set for your readers.

Whether you're doing it on purpose or not, you've already set standards for yourself.

There are a lot of places where you can set these expectations, like on the lead page (where you told the reader what they would get), in your first emails (where you told the reader what to expect as a subscriber), and even in your past emails.

Managing Expectations:

1. How often you send emails

In this case, if you said you'd send one email a week, but now you send one every day, that's going to hurt open rates because people don't expect it.

NOTE: The frequency does not matter, as long as your readers expect that frequency to be the same as what you promised. It's important to figure out how often you want to send out mail. Then, let your readers know what to expect from you.

2. The subject line is relevant to the content

If your subscribers come to believe that your email headlines are not relevant, they'll stop opening them. You can train them to open by making sure your subject lines are always aligned with the message.

3. Your content is relevant to the reason they subscribed

I recently purchased a product from someone I'd never come across before. The product was fine. I also received an email, like so:

"Last call...
Alright, due to a popular demand for a webbie replay
Here we go - it won't be there for long [1]
On this webbie we show you how to turn e-books into money
Watch while you can
Have an awesome day"

As the topic was relevant to both the product I'd bought and my interests, I watched the replay.

Unfortunately, it had nothing to do with e-books. Instead it was a pitch for a trading bot.

When I emailed the vendor and asked for the correct link, he replied that was the correct link and that's what he is promoting.

I unsubscribed and he's lost a customer for good.

Tip: Recycling your list for stuff not relevant to why your subscribers signed up in the first places is sure to make people ignore your messages.

Make sure your subscribers know what they've signed up for right from the start, and keep to it.

Don't change it because you want to do something else. When you look at your tracking and testing data, you might not be happy with what it says.

Hold Your Reader's Interest

If your reader doesn't find value in the first paragraph, he'll move on. This is why your opener is so critical.

Nevertheless, the remainder must be equally captivating.

Think of your email like a trail of breadcrumbs.

The purpose of every word is to compel the reader to continue reading. Focus on refining your writing to keep the reader's attention.

Once you have a consistent voice for your emails you need to establish a message that is consistent throughout all of your marketing media, including emails.

This covers your brand message and what you're teaching your prospects and consumers.

It is easy to send mixed and contradictory signals, especially if you're an affiliate marketer or a general store promoting a lot of different things.

However, you need to assess whether your communications are delivering your brand and unique message – or trampling all over it.

Consider your identity and whether your emails are consistent not only over time, but also across platforms.

And if others are creating or contributing to your content, make sure they understand how you want your brand to be communicated through your messaging.

Conclusion

As you can see, a wide variety of factors determine whether or not your emails will be successful.

In **Chapters 1 – 3** we covered who you are, setting relevant, meaningful goals, and identifying your ideal subscriber.

In **Chapters 4 & 5** we talked about writing to and for that subscriber as an individual and developing your authentic voice.

Chapters 6 – 8 looked at the importance of strong subject lines, the challenges in writing emails people want to read, and how to make sure your communications are consistent with your brand.

You now have a guide that will help you identify and correct issues that hamper or hinder your email marketing.

Some things need patience (for example, developing a relationship with readers), while others require practice (such as crafting awesome subject lines).

However, take regular action and you will soon have a responsive list and see dramatic improvements in your results.

To your continued success

Paraic Bergin

paraicbergin.com

P.S. I've included 2 bonus chapters below – enjoy!

P.P.S. Check out https://paraicbergin.com/emails for a powerful course on writing emails that sell!

BONUS: NINE WAYS TO WRITE WINNING SUBJECT LINES

It's time to put everything you've just learned into practice.

Take a look at these 9 approaches, suitable for any niche. Feel free to swipe and change them to suit your needs...

The "Quick And Easy Solution"

People will open emails that promise solutions to their most pressing concerns, as you learned before.

But, guess what? They aren't looking for just any solution.

People will delete your email if you tell them they can lose weight but it will take them three years to accomplish so.

If you tell them that solving their problem will be difficult, they will look for a simpler solution.

People want solutions that are both rapid and easy to implement. This is why templates like this are useful:

Here's how to [obtain some benefit] quickly and easily...

E.G., Here's how you get rid of cellulite quickly and easily...

Here's another example of a template that uses this formula:

The quickest way to [get some benefit].

E.G., The simplest method I've found for losing 10 pounds quickly.

A Subject Line That Inspires Curiosity

The idea is to come up with a RELEVANT headline for your email.

Your readers will abandon you if the subject line isn't clearly relevant to the content (and will be unlikely to open future emails from you).

There are several techniques to pique people's interest in your subject line. Let me show you a couple of examples of templates:

[An ordinary object] that [accomplishes something extraordinary].

This popular plant, for example, boosts your metabolism!

[Astonishing result]?

"Lose weight without exercising?" for example.

Personalized Curiosity

This is where you combine customization with intrigue to

produce something that makes people want to click.

Do you know this [kind of] trick, [Name]?

E.G., "Hey Joe, do you know how to change a flat without getting your hands dirty?"

The "Urgent Freebie"

Scarcity (particularly in the form of urgency) is a strong motivator. This works wonders for increasing open rates on paid offers. You can, however, use it on free offerings as well.

We've combined the fear of losing out with a freebie in this example:
Before it's too late, [get your free offer]!

"Download this free program before it's gone forever!" for example.

Another template that uses this formula is:

Get [thing] for free while you can - offer expires shortly

E.G., Take advantage of your free copywriting consultation while you still can — time is running out!

The Social Proof Subject Line

This is the subject line that implies that other people are benefiting, and that the reader should act (i.e., open the email) if they wish to benefit as well.

Here's an example:

Is there anyone else interested in [a benefit]?

"Who else desires whiter teeth and a sexier smile?"

"Here's What Happened"

This is a subject line that hints at a story and, in most cases, catches the reader's interest enough to persuade them to click. Take a look at this template:

[I did something that the niche would be interested in.] This is what happened

E.G., "For two weeks, I just ate fruit." "This is what occurred..."

"Let's Do This Together"

Many people believe they have been dealing with their situation alone. Because you're all in this together, this subject line implies that you'll assist them.

For example:

Let's [earn some money] together...

"Let's work together to [improve your performance]"

a different template:

Allow me to assist you in [obtaining some benefit]..

"Let me help you shed those ten stubborn pounds."

The Special Offer

This not only gives a unique offer (which is motivating), but it can also add a time limit to generate a sense of urgency or scarcity.

Here's a non-urgent template:

Now is the time to order [Product] and [receive something else for free]...

E.G., "Get this meal planning app for free when you order the fat loss guide!"

Here's an example of a template with a sense of urgency:

Your unique [kind of discount] is about to expire...

"Your special 50% discount on all software expires soon..."

The Expert

People want to follow specialists and authority in a niche, as you learned previously in this article. And you can take advantage of that fact by using this subject line template to boost your open rate:

What [some specialists] know about [obtaining a benefit]...

E.G., Doctors' advice on how to get rid of back discomfort.

Now for the final component in increasing the number of people who open your emails...

BONUS: TRACKING & TESTING

What gets measured gets done - Peter Drucker

In an ideal world, all goals would be measurable and outcomes measured against goals. In reality, we often neglect it.

What get measured and reported improves exponentially - Pearson's Law

It is vitally important to measure the right things and to control what can be controlled.

It is equally important to avoid measuring the wrong things and trying to control what is beyond our control.

Useful Metrics Are:

- # subscribers
- # unsubscribes
- # subscriber churn

- # complaints (and your response to those)
- # response rates (and your response to those)
- % Click-thru rates
- $ cost of new subscribers
- $ cost of email maintenance
- $ revenue per subscriber
- $ lifetime value of subscriber
- $ value of list building investment
- Return on Investment (ROI)

Why You Should Test And Track

There are industry 'norms' for email performance. But each subscriber list is different and composed of individual people. While there may be averages measured across millions of subscribers, your averages will be unique to your list.

So you are competing against yourself.

To do this effectively, you should test your efforts and track your results. In other words, let hard evidence (rather than "gut feelings") guide your judgments instead of the other way around.

When something works, keep doing it. If something has potential, experiment to see if you can make it better.

If you something is ineffective, discard it and try something else.

The main email service providers have built-in statistics that you may use to track the effectiveness of your campaigns.

The key actions you'll be tracking are:

(a)   Open rates
      Caution here – with increased privacy concerns, reported open rates may be significantly lower than actual, depending on the device used.
(b)   click-through rates, i.e. the number of clicks.

What Should You Test?

A wide variety of factors influence whether or not individuals read your email and click on your links. Only a few of them (such as subject lines) can be directly tested, so they are the ones you should concentrate on.

Global Factors

These are issues that may impact on your results, independently of the content of your emails.

Your Email Service Provider (Esp)

I recommend you only use an ESP who can give you decent in-built tracking and testing capabilities.

Unfortunately, not all ESP's do.

The second key question to consider is deliverability - will your emails reach the mailbox of your intended recipient?

1. What is the email service provider's (ESP) uptime like?

You'll have trouble having your emails delivered if your ESP has a lot of service outages. If you're trying to send emails at a specific time of day, for example, you can be off by many hours if the service is down.

2. What is the deliverability rate of the email service

provider?

The best email service providers work hard to ensure that your emails get in the correct inboxes. ESPs that place a high importance on deliverability will usually have a dedicated team working on it.

"From" Field

Does the reader recognize your name / brand / company name / domain name (i.e. what is in the "from" field).

A common mistake is when a subscriber joins your 'NAME' list but you are sending email from a different name.

When your subscriber doesn't associate the 'from' name with the site or identity they signed up with:

- Your emails don't get opened
- Unsubscribes increase
- You get spam complaints.

If you're having trouble increasing open or click rates while experimenting with subject lines and offers, you may want to assess whether you've established a trusting relationship with your readers.

NOTE: You can attempt to improve on the other aspects (such as creating a relationship with your readers) with each email you send, but it's really difficult to test the factor directly.

Date And Time

The best time to send an email is when your readers are active, online, and have the time to click on your emails.

Without testing, you won't know for sure which days and times are the best.

Look at your statistics to see if there is a time when most of your subscribers joined. This will be a good guideline to follow.

If a lot of people joined at 9:00am on weekdays, you can start testing that time to measure responses.

If your subscribers are mostly from one region, aligning your schedule with that time zone makes sense.

Otherwise, assume your readers are on EST and work from there.

Mobile-Friendly

__Most__ of your subscribers will see your emails on their cell phones. HTML emails should be checked for compatibility with smartphones and tablets.

Your click-thru-rate will be low if your email can't be read on a mobile device.

**HINT:**   Always prepare a plain text version as well as HTML

Email Layout

Large passages of text can be a laborious read, and many people are unwilling to put in the effort.

Use simple language and brief sentences. Your message should have a lot of white space so it's easy to read.

Break up long emails with bolded sub-headlines.

A good way to break up big paragraphs is to use bulleted lists.

Sometimes, incorporating visuals will help break up the content and make it more appealing. With long emails or ones that include a lot of data, this can be quite useful.

These Are The Major, Testable Elements To Pay Attention To:

- The subject line.
- The opening sentence.
- The offer (both the product and the price)
- The call to action
- The PS (some people will skip right to the end).
- When and how often you send emails.

Email Subject Line

Here's one of the most important things:

- Have you come up with a subject line that catches the reader's attention and makes them want to open your email?

The subject line of your e-mail should be interesting. And short.

Make sure your email headline packs a big punch in 50 characters or less.

Opening Sentence

Just as your subject line is the headline of this form of sales letter, your opening sentence is your sub-headline.

The purpose of each part of your message is to lead the reader to the conclusion, i.e. your call to action.

Make sure your opener is a natural follow-on from the subject line and drives the reader onto the rest of the email.

Offers And Pricing

Target the right market with the right product at the right pricing.

Your click-thru rates will suffer if any of these are out of whack.

To find the appropriate product at the right pricing for the right audience:

- find out what's already selling in your niche
- segment your list and test different offers

Call To Action (Cta)

The goal of your email is to have the reader take an action.

Is your message focused and targeted in a way that organically leads to your call to action?

Test different formats for your call to action

Signature And Post Script (Ps)

Your signature reinforces your brand and identity. Your P.S. helps anchor it in the reader's mind.

The P.S. is the 3rd most read part of your email, after the headline and opener. This is because many people skip the body and want to get 'to the point'.

Not having a P.S. is like leaving money on the table. It's prime real estate that could, and should, bring in revenue.

Focus On One Thing

When testing and tracking, keep in mind that you should only focus on and test **ONE** factor at a time. That way, if conversion rates vary when you're testing, you'll know it's because of the factor you're testing.

Let's say you're researching the effect of email subject lines on open and click-through rates.

In this situation, the subject lines should be the only thing that differs between the emails you send. The rest of the variables should be kept the same.

For example, if you send half of your emails at different times of the day, you've simply added another variable to your equation.

If your conversion rates differ across the two testing groups, you won't be able to tell if it's because of the subject lines... or the fact that you sent the emails at two distinct times of the day.

To put it another way, keep all other variables constant.

Conclusion

As you can see, a wide variety of factors affect your results.

We've covered the main global issues, including ESP, your name recognition, timing your emails, being mobile friendly and message layout.

We've also looked at the primary in-message items from your subject line, opening phrase/sentence, CTA, signature and PS.

And the golden rule – test only one variable at a time.

Focus on these and watch your results improve dramatically!

ABOUT THE AUTHOR

Paraic Bergin

Paraic Bergin started his career as a Chartered Certified Accountant with KPMG in Ireland and went on to work in the UK, the Middle East and Asia. With over 20 years experience in marketing and business development consulting, he specializes in helping small and medium-sized businesses adapt to the rapidly changing commercial environment, especially in the area of digital marketing.

This is his fourth book.

www.ingramcontent.com/pod-product-compliance
Lightning Source LLC
Chambersburg PA
CBHW071953120726
48001CB00005B/2164